How to Become a More Effective Teacher of Minority Students

by Dr. Azel C. Colston Jr.

DORRANCE
PUBLISHING CO
EST. 1920
PITTSBURGH, PENNSYLVANIA 15238

Dorrance Publishing Co., Inc.
585 Alpha Drive
Suite 103
Pittsburgh, PA 15238
Visit our website at *www.dorrancebookstore.com*

ISBN: 978-1-4809-1009-6
eISBN: 978-1-4809-0847-5

THE (FINAL PROJECT)
OF
AZEL C. COLSTON, JR.
is approved, and acceptable
in content, quality, and form.

CENTURY UNIVERSITY
2155 Louisiana Blvd. N.E.
Albuquerque, New Mexico 87110

(July - 1993)

"How to Become a More
Effective Teacher of
Minority Students"

By

(Azel Carl Colston, Jr.)

(Dissertation)

Submitted in partial fulfillment
of the requirement for the degree of
Doctor of Philosophy in Education

Century University
2155 Louisiana Boulevard, N.E.
Albuquerque, New Mexico 87110
(July, 1993)

ABSTRACT

Having taught minority students approximately twenty-three years, there were times when the thought of leaving the educational profession became prevalent because of such difficult problems and unforeseen circumstances. However, I am a firm believer that even in our rapidly changing society where problems are inevitable, there must be that special teacher who can relate to, give positive feedback, and motivate even the most disaffected child in the classroom.

I have reluctantly listened to numerous educators complain about problems concerning many minority students. It is unequivocally clear: in order to become a more effective teacher of minority students, there must be a genuine concern for them and their academic success. The teacher must concern himself with the "total" development of the child.

Therefore, I decided to formulate this doctoral project with the idea of investigating modalities, strategies, and techniques to assist teachers in becoming more effective and caring while teaching minority students.

It is the teachers' responsibility to accept the challenge of educating all students to the best of their ability. Excuses have been made long enough. It is time for us to assist our students in every way possible by providing an academic atmosphere which will allow children the opportunity to actualize and maximize their potential.

HOW TO BECOME A MORE EFFECTIVE TEACHER OF MINORITY STUDENTS

ACKNOWLEDGEMENTS

It is appropriate that Dr. Frederick H. Kingdon be acknowledged in this paper as one who served not only as faculty advisor, but also a mentor, as well.

I would also like to thank my good friend, Leslie Ormond, for all his support and encouragement during this study.

TABLE OF CONTENTS

HOW TO BECOME A MORE EFFECTIVE TEACHER OF MINORITY STUDENTS INTRODUCTION SCOPE AND PURPOSE OF THE STUDY

The association of teacher personality and changes in pupil creativity is a major concern of teacher education and is well documented in casual and scholarly publications, in government reports, and in international studies.

The traditional role of the classroom teacher is to impart information and skills to his students. It is not feasible, however, for a teacher to limit himself to merely academic concerns. Children are multi-dimensional: they are capable of a wide range of behaviors, of which the intellectual and academic represent only a part. Unfortunately, many non-academic problems of children are ignored by teachers so long as they don't interfere with the normal orderly process on the school.

One notable exception, however, is aggressive behavior. Children who behave aggressively quickly become the focus of a teacher's attention and are then subject to whatever means the relevant authority (teacher, administrator, guidance person) believes suitable to solve the problem. These may range from administrative-typed solutions such as suspending the student, or calling parent conferences, child-study team intervention, to efforts at dealing with the child directly–either by simple reprimand and punishment, or (where such service is available) by referral to a counselor or psychologist. Typically, however, the teacher does not attempt to use his or her expertise in the areas of teaching and learning to solve the problems of undesirable emotional behavior.

Despite this attitude about the dis-relation of behaviors such as aggression and learning, there is a growing body of psychological knowledge which relates learning processes to the development and maintenance of emotional behavior. As professionals in the field of learning, teachers should be aware of potential means at their disposal for handling and identifying problems that can affect learning or that are affected by learning; in this case, the problem is one of aggressive behavior. The purpose of this study is to investigate the relationships which have been uncovered between learning and aggression, and to investigate possible applications that this knowledge might have to control aggressive behavior.

DEFINITION OF TERMS:

Aggression is defined behaviorally and is to include assaults on other children and adults, episodes of thievery, firesetting, constant classroom disruptions, and verbal hostility.[i]

Some of the forms of aggression which may be manifest have been classified as: early responses of diffuse, chaotic emotional outburst; indirect attacks such as destroying possessions, engaging in behavior calculated to annoy, threats, tattling, etc.; indirect aggression by derogatory remarks and rumor-mongering; or attempts to punish others by self-destruction. This latter category may include action against family in the forms of public immortality, criminality, and delinquency.[ii]

Learning is defined as an observable change in behavior that can be attributed to practice.[iii] Cultural Deprivation is defined as the unavailability to a child of the usual accountment of his culture. These include adequate exposure to the social, intellectual, and artistic achievements of the culture; versatility in the behavior norms of the culture; and culturally normal levels of nutrition and health care.[iv]

Roe, (1956); Super (1957); Holland (1959); and Tiedman and O'Hara, (1963), were all interested in using personality variables in explaining vocational behavior. However, the nature of this relationship is not clearly understood. Many of their studies were descriptive of the nature of occupations or personality variables in explaining the attitudes presumably associated with occupations.[v] It has not been made entirely clear why particular occupations have been chosen for study, nor how the various insights and implications gained from their research been converted into explicit hypotheses and subjected to testing.

The public needs to become aware of the need for developing schools which develop wholesome personalities in children and teachers alike. Teachers in educational institutions should also become involved and tackle the responsibility of predicting which of the novice teacher will experience success in the schools.

PURPOSE

I am trying to determine:

1) Which of the psychological needs, attitudes, prejudices, conflicts, and personal and social values of the teacher are translated into the behavior patterns which become the potent influence on a pupil's social growth.

Also:

2) To determine the way for the development of materials which can predict teacher behavior.

We realize, for the most part, that schools are one of the most important institutions we have available to us. However, all too often the American system of education has been deemed a failure. Much too often a child will enter into a school bursting with enthusiasm and curiosity, only to leave it dampened by what he has encountered there. The constant criticism of our system as it stands has led the way towards a low-keyed reform movement in American schools, starting with the teachers.

In today's society, the students are expected to have positive, cooperative, mature, energetic, and dedicated attitudes towards their peers and those in authority. The first question that enters my mind is what kind of teacher should the child be exposed to. The teacher chosen should best be able to foster those attitudes mentioned above. The teacher should also be able to provide those types of experiences which will insure maximum growth, time and time again.

Children come to school with a need to know just what the world is all about. They also come in order to gain an understanding as to how things are done, where they come from, how they're put together, and a desire to master tricks of the adult world such as the magic of the written word and using numbers.

A teacher who is mature, accepting, and friendly will know that the children are not always able to manage the job of self control by themselves. This type of instructor will realize that it is his or her goal to become for the child an interesting as well as interested person.

Limitations: This research is limited to a critical analysis of studies and written professional opinions of an unempirical nature.

Delimiting the Problem: This study is concerned with applications of knowledge about learning to problems of children's aggressive behavior. It will not involve itself with problems of isolated aggression or with levels of aggressive behavior that are not high enough to present a problem.

Assumptions: The reader should note that this paper represents only a partial review of the relevant literature; the author believes, however, that the sources used are representative of the field as a whole.

Hypothesis: It is hypothesized that aggression is:

a) in at least some cases a result of learning;

b) at least partially treatable by appropriate learning.

Thus, since a teacher is a learning professional, he may use his expertise in the non-academic area of behavioral modification, as well as in the traditional subject matter.

Statement of the Problem: Can teachers use their knowledge about learning to reduce aggressive behavior in problem children?

Review of the Literature

There are several references which point out that teacher characteristics are distinctly associated with changes in pupil behavior. Before I go into theories, something should be said about the importance of attitudes in the teacher-pupil relationship.

As we know, a certain person's attitudes are much more likely to be apparent to someone close to him than they appear to himself. Perhaps not always evident to us, a person's attitudes are a controlling force in a person's decision-making process. We are usually elusive about our own attitudes. There, an analysis of one's attitude is often a difficult task, if not an almost impossible one. The type of exploration that Rogers developed with his client-centered therapy can sometimes be accompanied by attitude change because of the detachment of the psychoanalyst. In such a technique it is necessary to look at one's actions as objectively as is possible. Hopefully, the drives and motivations leading to the actions will be identified.[vi] As a result of this particular therapy, the subject becomes more self accepting and free. In general, the self becomes liberated when the person is able to detect the action structured that had been imposed upon him by the attitudes he has acquired.

The basic problem takes its appearance when an untrained person tries to fathom the attitudes of another. If the attitudes turn out to be much the same as those of the evaluator, it might appear that no attitude is involved. The evaluator tends to accept the decisions of the other person on the basis what they both see reality in the same manner. However, if the person evaluated acts or behaves in a perverse way, then the evaluator may assume that the person is merely acting out of stupidity or nonconformity. The onlooker may give little thought to the possibility of a differing attitude.

Sometimes, teachers are apt to fall into this particular interpretation of student response patterns. Whenever teachers and students share the same attitudes, action interpretations are likely to be similar. However, when backgrounds appear to be dissimilar, differences in attitudes often lead the way to serious misunderstandings. Difficulties in the classroom will often take place because teachers and students have differing ideas about such issues as homework, or even the relevance of the particular lesson taught. In each of these circumstances, the student or the teacher interprets the action in terms of his own attitude. For example, a student might see a particular problem as being much less disrespectful or less threatening than does the teacher. For the most part, the public is not educated to the importance of the thought or ideas that precede most actions. Even if a person is aware of this fact, the casual factors are still sometimes rather difficult to unravel. In general, a person's own attitudes color his interpretation of another's attitudes. The stronger he feels about his own beliefs, then the more distorted his perceptions of another's will be. The distance between viewpoints will increase with the heightening of emotions. A strong attitude of rejection toward people can be diminished when the person begins to look at certain actions as phrases rather than as threats.

The energy with which a person can reject certain situations is an indication of the strength of his attitudes toward them. In more informal evaluation, a person is judged by the way he acts.

Another problem in evaluating the attitudes of others is the idea of conformity. This is particularly evident if a person does not hold an attitude with strong convictions. As a result, an observer may misinterpret his actions on non-existent motives. A person's true attitudes come through when the forces of conformity are withdrawn. For example, a person better expresses himself when in the company of family and friends.

There has been a fluctuation of systemic teaching of attitudes in the United States. For years, it seems that the objective of our educational system was to teach immigrants the attitude of loyalty to this country. If the teaching of attitudes is to again become one of our primary goals, then the same care must be given to defining desirable attitudes that are given to the teaching of other skills, such as reading or history. In other words, the teacher must plan for this facet of teaching in much the same way as he plans for cognitive learning.

During the fifties, teachers were generally committed to teaching goals that distinguished between attitudes, skills, and understandings (Lee & Lee, 1950). In general, educational goals presumed some evaluation of what was learned with reference to some sort of stated purpose. Many of the goals for teaching attitudes have been stated in terms so vague that a serious evaluation was deemed impossible.

On the other hand, during the sixties, two panels of evaluation specialists classified educational goals with a good deal of precision. This was to make possible the testing of gains that the student made. It was also decided that the cognitive and affective sides of education in the classroom setting need not be divorced from each other. Perhaps we can say that attitudes are learned in most any subject, but the development of constructive attitudes are dependent on the teacher, along with his or her intention to direct this learning through constructive channels.

This appears to be several references that point out teacher characteristics are distinctly associated with changes in pupil behavior. Beside teacher characteristics, the method by which teaching is carried on is also of the utmost importance. Stressing the latter, Jerome Bruner contends that the overall intellectual development of young children can be sped up in several ways. First of all, the teacher should introduce appropriate materials in the classroom setting. Secondly, correct instructional methods should be employed. Also, a strong curriculum is necessary. Bruner believed that with use of such methods, a child will be tempted to "explore and discover underlying principles that will move him into the higher stages of cognitive development."[vii]

The next two studies involve the emotional involvement of the teacher as well as the amount of self understanding that the teacher has regarding himself. Whenever the effort is made to promote the very concept of self understanding in the classroom, one of the most impressive effects is the emotional impact that this work has upon the teacher. A familiar classroom setting reveals that pupils will reveal a great range of emotional problems whenever given the uninhibited circumstance to do so. In any cases a child, or perhaps the entire group, will release a tremendous measure of feeling. In the classroom where the children have been termed "problems" and where they have been kicked around the school system as well as at home, there is likely to be a display of emotions. The hostility and despair presented by students is likely to have a staggering and discouraging effect of the teacher. Sometimes, the anxiety that is shown can rise to such proportions that the whole episode can be a frightening experience for the teacher. The grievances that are revealed may have a bitter attachment not quite like anything the teacher has experienced before.

A display such as this can result in a threatening situation. Many times the teacher may be somewhat "overwhelmed by the terrific needs that are laid bare."[viii] Some of these needs may appear to be so great that the teacher sees his own abilities as quite limited. Oftentimes, the situation appears hopeless.

The teacher's character will undergo feelings of insecurity especially if there is a high degree of expectation on himself. Such a degree of expectation would pressure the instructor to find an immediate solution to the problem. This, naturally, is an unrealistic demand. Feelings of guilt and frustration are likely to ensue.

Perhaps another sore spot in teaching would be the idea of similarity of situation. Many times the problems presented by the student are likely to touch upon the teacher's own unresolved problems. We tend to lose sight of the fact that they are human beings just as the student.

Also, emotional problems may result because the teacher is apt to place demands upon himself. Many of these demands may be severe and unrealistic. It may occur that he tries to remain immune to emotional problems and their effects. This, of course, is ridiculous in that people in general find it almost impossible to be concerned with others' emotional problems without becoming involved themselves. In dealing with a child who has such problems, the teacher might expect to be able to reach the child in time. A highly competent psychologist may not be able to cope with this child, but the teacher may not wish to consider this particular limitation. Of course, this is where the difficulty lies.

Because of emotional involvement of one form or another, a teacher may decide to try his hand at teaching courses dealing with psychological problems. One teacher who was involved in such study commented that it was restful to go back and teach some sort of academic subject after having wrestled with the problems of a led group.[ix]

Teachers will differ in the extent to which they become involved beyond their capacity to endure, and in the extent to which they demand more of themselves than is reasonable. As a result, some teachers are going to be better suited to their job with relation to temperament and disposition.

However, even when the teacher who is well suited to his job goes to work, he will continue to undergo pressure daily. There will be times when work is frustrating, and he may have some serious doubts about his ability to perform as an instructor. This doubt can be caused by several factors. However, one significant drawback might be the criticism that the teacher is likely to come across from parents and pupils, as well as other teachers.

Therefore, it seems important that a teacher can obtain a certain amount of appreciation in order to maintain some sort of morale. A significant source of this help would come from fellow teachers. Group meetings involving these teachers would seem to remedy the situation to the extent that feelings could be shared. Perhaps, then, at these meetings, some viable solutions could be worked out.

A word should now be asked on the force of the self concept in relation to the teacher's work. The basic idea of self concept in education may initially strike the teacher in a negative way. It may seem that adopting such a principle would merely add to his workload. But in the long run this is not the case, for it actually enhances the job of teaching. In one sense, it may eliminate the feelings of futility that many teachers today confront. More especially so on the high school level, it will liberate the teacher from the need to constantly justify himself in whatever it is he is teaching.

According to one writer, "the self concept offers teachers a principle which integrates the basic features of their personality."[x] He believes that without this in mind, all of daily life seems fragmented and futile. However, without this total idea of self concept there can be no involvement. And, in essence, isn't this the abstract personality trait which is the basis of all teaching.

In a similar respect, the more that a teacher can see his work as fitting into a "total" framework, the simpler it will be for him to tackle the details of his work. Now that he has achieved this idea of self concept, he no longer has to rationalize his work. Now he is able to put his energy into creative endeavors. A better rapport will develop between himself and the students involved. Teaching will take on a perspective he has never thought possible. In summary, the greater the amount of self concept as well as self involvement, the better able a teacher is equipped to understand each student's struggle to acquire an identity.

The next concept deals with teacher self understanding; an idea working hand in hand with self concept. We can assume that a good part of education lies in the task of leading the student to a better self understanding. If this is possible, then we must make the assumption that the teacher, too, needs this understanding and should be able to accept help in coming to this realization.

As a starting point, there should be a greater emphasis on the time of teacher training best suited to the individual's needs. If this turns out to be effective, a greater amount of wisdom will be offered as the teacher works with his students, and he will be able to examine and evaluate the implications of what he is trying to do.[xi]

The type of teacher who characteristically throws himself into his work will find himself in the midst of self examination over and over again. If the person involved is basically an insecure person, these confrontations are apt to be a painful and threatening experience. However, if the teacher is a stable individual, then this type of experience is likely to be an extremely rewarding one.

In other words, in trying to make the student learn, the teacher is learning much himself. It is even possible that he will learn more than a student in the course of a year. Similarly, by helping others, the teacher is plotting for himself a rewarding experience.

Perhaps another source of increasing self understanding can be found in relationships with other teachers. We have already mentioned that these relationships will encourage morale. Cooperation is necessary if different views are to be aired. With a new slant on things, teachers will, perhaps, be able to settle disputes in his own classroom situation.

One problem concerning qualifications that a teacher comes across is "the best kind of balance that a teacher might strike in his capacity for emotional involvement and in his capacity for intellectual conceptualization of his work."[xii] With relation to this idea, one writer sees four rather broad categories into which teachers may fit when judged from the point of view of their ability to understand their pupils, to better relate themselves to them, and to help "the student understand himself."[xiii]

First, there is the teacher who can say but can't do. He is the teacher who knows several abstract theories and concepts but is rendered helpless when the time comes to relate them to his pupils. Neither is he capable of relating himself to their concerns in a way that makes any difference to them. He "has the language," but he is emotionally detached. There is no chance for him to really communicate with his students.

Second, there is the teacher who can't say but can do. This teacher has the great capacity to work with his students and can also greatly appreciate their feelings. However, his flaw lies in the fact that he is unable to interpret exactly what he is doing in terms of theories or principles of human behavior.

Third in this subjective interpretation is the teacher who can't say and can't do. Obviously, this is a considerable drawback. Briefly, this teacher has neither "the verbal theory nor the emotional substance."[xiv]

Finally, there is the teacher who can both say and do. This teacher not only can experience the feelings of the group but is also able to articulate these feelings. In summary, he not only can "realize an emotional experience, but is also able to conceptualize it—and he does it whenever it seems to help the learning process."[XV]

We have to assume that no teacher will conform to any of these categories in all or no way. Although the ideal instructor seems to be the one who can both say and do, the other three examples do their purpose. The teacher who is able to say but cannot do may sometimes accomplish something by his mastery of words. He may be able to communicate some idea to some student who up to that point has not been able to articulate for himself. In a sense, this teacher may be responsible for some sort of chain reaction in that he can provide answers on the verbal level. He is able to relay certain thoughts although he himself may not be aware of their significance.

The teacher who can do but cannot say might also be performing a valuable service. However, the more unsure he is on an underlying principle, the more often he will find himself working according to chance.

Every now and then, one is bound to come across a teacher who seems to be doing a remarkable job on what might appear to be the intuitive level. But because of a lack of unification in principle, such a teacher will fail to make the most of a learning situation because of his lack of intellectual perception.

CHAPTER 2

HOW TO BE AN EFFECTIVE TEACHER

SECTION I:

In order to be an effective teacher, there is no doubt that one must have a thorough understanding and grasp of the environment around him. This environment not only includes the school culture itself and the technical aspects of education, but that of the community around the school.

In today's society there are so many factors that impact on the education of the student and the role of the teacher. There are children who come from broken homes, there are students who come from homes where both parents are working, and there are students who come from minority backgrounds. Each of these factors impact on the role of teaching, for these very factors influence the development of the child. Community and home environment are great influences on a child's ability to learn, how they respond to education in general, and their attitudes towards the teacher. In order for a teacher to be effective, a teacher must grasp completely where each and every student comes from. The teacher must be aware if the student comes from an impoverished home, the teacher must understand the cultural heritage of his students, and the teacher must understand and know about the community in general from which the student comes.

If a teacher understands the background of a student, then he can effectively utilize the professional skills he has acquired in reaching the student and providing quality education.

When a person undertakes the task of teaching, the first step that must be taken is an evaluation of self. The teacher must look at him- or herself objectively and face up to their own strengths and weaknesses. For example, if a white teacher gets a job teaching in a ghetto community, the first step that the teacher must take is evaluating his or her own prejudices. If a teacher is prejudiced, or has preconceived notions about the students they teach, then the teacher will not be an effective teaching professional. Being honest with oneself means that then they can face up to their fears and prejudices and try to correct them. It must be pointed out that preconceived notions and prejudices can work in reverse as well, when a minority teacher gets a job in an all-white neighborhood.

The key to being a successful teacher is being one that has the ability to take criticism, criticize oneself, and be objective in all circumstances. There is nothing more harmful than a teacher writing off a student's ability merely because of their background.

An example of such preconceptions is the story of a ten-year-old boy in Albuquerque, New Mexico. This boy had great anxieties when it came to performance in school. He had a teacher who automatically had a low opinion of him and his academic ability, merely because he was of Hispanic extraction. The teacher did not work with the child merely because of his Hispanic origins. This teacher entered his job with a built-in prejudice that just because someone spoke Spanish, with English as a second language, that they would not be able to perform well in school. From the start of the school year, the teacher had a low opinion of the boy's academic ability. As a result, the boy suffered great anxiety and had problems performing well in school. Once the boy was removed from this hostile environment, he performed very well in school. It must be noted that the problem this boy from New Mexico faced was in no way an isolated case. The boy faced a problem common among Spanish-speaking Americans who want to be part of the United States but want to retain their native values, customs, and language.[xvi]

This story is an example, of why it is extremely important for a teacher to know himself before entering the teaching profession. A teacher's fears, prejudices, and preconceptions can do more harm to a student than anyone can imagine. Therefore, it is extremely important for any teacher to be honest with oneself and overcome handicaps that can be potentially dangerous to a student's education, self-esteem, and development. Otherwise, the harm inflicted upon the child will be carried with the student through the rest of his life.

Other aspects that must be taken under consideration by a teacher in understanding his students is the community they come from, the home environment of the student, the cultural heritages of the student, and the cultural heritages of the student population which they encounter in their daily tasks.

Poverty, discrimination, social status, and home environment all impact upon the child's psyche, self-esteem, and ability to learn. The good teacher will learn all he can about the students in his domain. Take all factors into consideration and work as hard as possible to overcome whatever handicaps these students may possess in order to provide them with a quality education.

One of the major problems in this country is the poverty level of students in urban areas. One must understand, if a child goes to sleep hungry, the child will not be able to function properly in a school environment. How the community deals with poverty, along with the Federal Government, not only affects the individual, but the school culture as well.

The present welfare system, many believe, is not effective. There have been many proposals to reform. However, the loss is on the children. If children who come from welfare homes see that their parents are trying to lift themselves out of this dismal situation, they can get a sense of pride and purpose. If a child is shown a positive attitude and a desire to work, then the child may see a ray of hope. There must be some motivation for a child. Granted, the teacher must provide some of the motivation, but it is important that this motivation come not only from within the school, but the community and the Federal Government.

There are some programs being introduced that will reform the welfare system. One of the programs being considered is the workforce models, under which those who receive welfare must work for their payments. This type of program is much more successful among those who already have skills. It must be pointed out, though, that many welfare recipients are single mothers who have few job skills and would need subsidies for day care and transportation to get to work. Therefore, some advocate an increase in block grants that will help the communities that need the most help. These block grants would serve as providing funds for job training, as well as extra funds for the educational system.[xvii]

There is much debate concerning how the welfare system is structured and what should be done to reform the system. The fact that does exist, though, is that the culture of poverty that characterizes America's underclass must be broken. Where it is true that welfare payments help sustain the underclass, doing away with the system would have disastrous consequences. The concept of workfare, which requires welfare recipients to work off their grants through state-assisted job training and placement, seems to be the more popular reform that exists. There are many problems with this type of program, where in many cases the programs are too "soft" with too many loopholes to do any large scale good. "Hard" workfare programs, which are often mandatory, suffer from similar structural flaws. A plan that solves many problems of conventional workfare would involve replacing cash-like welfare programs with an offer of employment from the government in a useful job at wages slightly lower than minimum wage. If a person worked, he or she would be paid. Those who didn't would be on their own. "This strategy would reinforce the work ethnic in the underclass culture."[xviii]

The above solution may seem harsh, but the reality of the situation is that the welfare system and welfare recipients are on a never-ending cycle. It is becoming a multi-generational phenomena, and this is where the role of educators, and their place in the community, comes into play. The teacher can enforce some sense of the work ethic in the students. However, the example many students receive at home affects their desire for learning. If they see that their parents are not working, that their grandparents, aunts, and uncles, all are on welfare, then a sense of hopelessness sets in. The student brings to question why they need an education. To these children of welfare recipients there seems to be no solution or way out of the poverty that they are experiencing and that their families have experienced for years. Therefore, not only is it up to the educator to motivate these children, instill them with hope, but it is the job of the government to find solutions that will end this never-ending cycle of poverty, not only for the betterment of the present generation, but for future generations as well.

It must be noted that the community itself can also help instill hope in children, as well. In fact, in one community, the Mt. Winans housing project, in Baltimore, the Federal Government, the city, and neighborhood, including the local schools, are working together on the project's renovation program. The neighborhood has found a new pride because the work is being done by local people. Residents of the housing project were trained in the skills and work attitudes necessary to do the renovation. "When completed, the renovation will have cost less than if it had been handled by a local contractor, and his work will be of equal or better quality."[xix]

Organizers chose a small, close-knit community and gained the support of its leaders early on. One of the project's economies, however, included setting the starting pay rate at the minimum wage, so, ironically, trainees who had been on welfare barely increased their gross income. "In spite of this, many continued the training, which reveals that many poor people will seize the chance to work when they can learn new skills."[xx]

As an educator, being involved in such programs and getting an understanding of the immediate community is extremely valuable in the long-run impact the educator can have on the student. This relates back to what we stated earlier concerning understanding oneself. One cannot assume that because someone is on welfare there is no hope for them and that they will be unaffected by the classroom environment; rather, a teacher who goes out to understand the community where he or she works may very well come across a community such as Mt. Winans, where a little push turns into something very constructive. Such a united community effort, by all in the community, is not lost upon the young. It is then the job of the educator to capitalize on such an experience in instilling hope and motivation into the young student. It is the wise teacher who will learn much about the community in which he or she works and use it to the advantage in educating the child.

Another aspect that can influence the teaching role is knowledge of the home environment of children that are not from welfare in this country; they have become known as "latchkey" children. Latchkey children are those who come home from school with neither of the parents at home, due to work obligations. Children who are left unsupervised at home can often be behavioral problems in the classroom. For this reason, it is imperative that a teacher and the school is aware of what children are in that position. Teachers, along with school administrators and community leaders, must work together with the parents to help supervise, in some way, the latchkey children. For example, educators, along with certain community centers, such as libraries, must form some sort of coalitions to provide children with more afternoon programs for the latchkey child. If the child has no one at home to go to, there is no reason why the educator cannot take advantage of the situation in the educational process. Libraries are becoming the home away from home for the thousands of "latchkey children" who have nothing to do after school. "As a result, the National Education Association is urging communities to provide their libraries with the additional resources necessary to cope with the influx."[xxi]

A study of children who must supervise themselves after school, conducted by sociologist Sandra Hoefferth and psychologist Virginia Cain, suggest that 2.1 million children age 5 to 13 years old are latchkey children. According to Hoefferth and Cain, 90 percent of the children are more than 9 years old, and the majority must fend for themselves for a maximum of two hours per day. Self-care is not more frequent among children from single parent homes, and mothers' employment situations did not consistently affect the decision to allow their children to supervise themselves. Hoefferth's and Cain's study revealed that most latchkey children are from well-educated, middle-to upper class families in suburban and rural areas.[xxii]

Regardless, though of the socio-economic background of the latchkey children, the fact remains that many children have problems coping with the phenomena. As a result, the child can become ambivalent, angry, and disruptive as a result of the lack of parental supervision. The role of the educator is quite important in such situations. If the teacher is aware of such a situation, certain projects can be given to these students to keep them occupied during the hours they are alone. There is no doubt that there can be some positive aspects for a child being left alone:

a growing sense of independence, a sense of self-worth, and growth in self-confidence. The teacher and the parent can work together, formulating some sort of curriculum in which the child and the parent will learn safety skills in self-care settings. This type of curriculum will allow parents to make proper decisions concerning the child's ability to stay alone, the guilt feelings will be alleviated, and the child becomes a participant in the decision-making process. This, along with exposure to the workplace for the child, will add to an understanding of why a child must be left alone. If the child visits the parent's workplace, not only will they gather an understanding of what the parent does for a living, but the child can better adapt to a mother's being gone all day if he can visualize where she is. "Seeing where a parent works gives a child a sense of pride."[xxiii]

Thus, what can be seen in this case is that if an educator understands the mechanisms of the different familiar structures within their classroom, they can be very instrumental in helping the student adapt to the school environment and to the environment the child faces outside of school. Through the use of community cooperation between educators, libraries, parents, and children, the educator can be the key in helping students adapt to the world around them. Using constructive educational tools, a child's familiar circumstances can be used in an advantageous way.

The last area which influences the teaching role is the differences and varieties of communities as a whole. More specifically, when a teacher undertakes the role of educator, he or she must be keenly aware of the needs, desires, and problems that may exist in, for example, the Black and Hispanic communities. For a teacher to be an effective educator, the teacher must be sensitive to the needs of these two communities.

In the case of the Hispanic community, one example was cited earlier. A teacher cannot have preconceptions about a student because of their Spanish heritage and their academic abilities, as cited in the case of the ten-year-old boy from New Mexico. There are problems that those of Hispanic origins face in their daily lives. The President of the Tomas Rivera Center in Clarement, California, in a speech to a group of educators, urged the educators to make a united effort to eliminate marginalization, exclusion, and alienation, and to ensure that U.S. institutions reflect diversity of the U.S. society. He spoke of such necessities in reciting the problems that he faced growing up as a member of minority group in the United States.

As an educator, one must understand that Hispanic-American culture embodies a dilemma: Hispanics want to be part of America but don't want to give up their past. The Latin American culture looks to the past, while the United States stands as the opposing new world experiment, offering the promise of rebirth and separation from the past. "Latin America, meanwhile, offers a fullness of life and a passion that America yearns for."[xxiv]

It is this dilemma, and ingrained prejudice by Americans, that the job of the educational system, and the educator, to integrate the various cultures and diversities that exist into the school curriculum. The teacher must recognize the validity of the heritage of all students' heritage and culture, integrate it into the classroom, and provide the Hispanic student, or other minority student, with a sense of pride and inclusion. Not only must curriculums include the diversity that exists in this country, but there must be an influx of minority educators into the system as well. "Teachers must be taught of the cultural heritages of their students, be taught how to make the students feel like they are part of the system, and how to encourage them to continue their educations, through the higher education system."[xxv]

The role of the educator is crucial in integrating the minority population into society as a whole. This cannot be accomplished unless the educator, the teacher, has a firm understanding and sensitivity to the needs of the student population with which they are entrusted.

The Black community faces many of the problems that the Hispanic community faces. Some of the problems that the Black community faces have been discussed earlier in dealing with students from welfare backgrounds. What is necessary for the Black student is more community involvement in the education of the Black child. The inner cities of the U.S. are plagued by decaying schools, high dropout rates, and students who are illiterate after graduation. Many blame the Reagan Administration for Federal cutbacks in funds for the problem, and others blame educators for ineffectiveness. In a study conducted by principals, good principal-teacher relationships, formal parental involvement, and flexible funding can be used for enrichment programs. In addition, a program developed by the Yale child study program and the New Haven School System found that low-income students achieved more if their teachers respected them and had confidence in their ability to learn. "Basically, this study, and other similar studies, have shown that educational performance of Blacks and other minorities can improve if there is cooperation among parents, teachers, and school administrators."[xxvi]

There is no doubt that, in evaluating the material gathered here, it is extremely important for a teacher to understand the environment in which he or she teaches. The modern educator faces thousands of variables in the workplace that influence the teaching process. There are too many to enumerate in this essay. Those not touched upon include drugs, health concerns, divorce, and other ethnic groups and their diversities. However, from addressing the few issues here, one can understand the scope of difficulty involved in being an effective teacher. It is clear that it is imperative that a teacher have an understanding and sensitivity to the needs of the students in his or her care. The teacher must understand the community from which they come, the cultural backgrounds, the socio-economic backgrounds, and the home environment from which these students come from. If the teacher can accomplish this, then the teacher can be an effective educator, motivating and encouraging students in their educational pursuits.

SECTION III: LITERACY

"We are creating a new generation of illiterates." With those words, Robert Barnes, an official at the U.S. Department of Education, released a chilling analysis of a basic literacy test given to 3,400 Americans age 20 and over. Thirteen percent flunked the test, able to answer only 20 or fewer of the 26 multiple choice questions.[xxvii] From the results of this test, Barnes projects that 17 million to 21 million adult Americans are unable to read. Blame it on the U.S. school system and on the government, which locates only 17 dollars a person for hard-core adult illiterates. Though Barnes admits that volunteer organizations are doing a good job, the number of people entering the illiteracy pool each year equals roughly the number that are helped.[xxviii]

The composition of the estimated 17 to 21 million U.S. illiterates breaks down as follows:

Eight percent come from rural areas, 41% from metropolitan areas, and 51% from small towns and suburbs. The racial and ethnic breakdown is: English speaking whites: 41%; Black: 22%; Spanish-speaking: 22%; and other Non-English speaking individuals: 15%. The age breakdown is as follows: "20 to 39: 40%; 40 to 59: 28%; and 60 and older: 32%."[xxix]

What the above statistics are indicative of is that the problem of illiteracy is growing with the younger generation. This could be due to higher dropout rates among the younger population or the deterioration of the school system due to cuts in federal and local spending. The fact is that these figures are based on a test that measured only the inability to read, with no attempt to establish the number of U.S. adults who, although technically literate, cannot read well enough to function as successful citizens. Many experts believe that a measure of functional literacy would have even more disheartening results. Indeed, a study by the University of Texas in 1975 suggested that "one in five Americans cannot read well enough to perform the simplest tasks. Of 15,000 tested, 20 percent could not write a check without an error so serious that a bank could not cash it; 22 percent were unable to address an envelope well enough to ensure postal delivery; 40 percent could not figure correct change from a store purchase; and more than half had at least some trouble with reading or writing."[xxx]

The total cost of illiteracy to the U.S. economy cannot be accurately measured, but critics insist the nation is paying dearly in lost productivity and in human misery. Reports tell of an industrial worker killed because he could not read a warning sign, a sick child given a pink detergent instead of stomach medicine by a mother who could not decipher the bottle labels, and "another mother who endorsed what she thought was a routine permission slip for a field trip only to discover that she had relegated her daughter to a home for the retarded."[xxxi]

The statistics involved with the lack of the literate capabilities of the American people are astounding. The impact of illiteracy can be felt both in the schools and outside the schools. The impact on the schools themselves is the actual burden of the school system to educate the illiterate. It is obvious that it is the job of the educators to ensure that students graduate literate, but now the burden upon the school system is to educate those who have already passed through the educational system and have graduated functionally illiterate. One cannot underestimate the impact of illiteracy upon society as a whole, as well as the individual.

The costs associated with illiteracy in the United States involves not only funding by the government for literacy programs, but costs of welfare and unemployment benefits paid to those who cannot read. The monies spent on people who are functionally illiterate amount to $3.6 billion in taxpayers' money each year "according to one literacy report, Jonathan Kozol."[xxxii]

E.D. Hirsch, author of *What Every American Needs to Know*, contends that schools no longer teach the information that a citizen needs to be a participant in his community. He blames John Dewey's "progressive" theory of education and its modern day successors, which contend reading and writing skills need not be tied to specific content. He concludes with a list of some five thousand items defining what culturally literate Americans should know. "Hirsch is an advocate of the old school of learning and blames modern educators for the dilemma now facing American society."[xxxiii]

The fact is that Mr. Hirsch may be overreacting concerning the benefits of the modern educational system. While he may think the earlier educational systems were more successful in preparing citizens for "Life in the Community," he ignores the fact that in past generations rudimentary skills were considered adequate. One cannot deny that millions of

Americans are functionally illiterate, lacking the reading skills needed to keep pace with the demands of living in the information age. "But the fact is, though, Americans have always held reading and writing in high regard; the level of skills required in the past are just not adequate to keep up with a society advancing in technological terms."[xxxiv] Therefore one cannot totally blame Dewey's "progressive" educational methods, but rather can only blame the educational system's inability to keep up with the rapidly changing demands being made of the citizens of this country.

The problem of illiteracy in the United States, though, is not being ignored. Though it is not the prime national goal, it should be, and that goal should be to teach every citizen to read and write as quickly and as pleasurably as possible, because people who cannot read are handicapped in an essential sense. Three changes in reading instruction at the earliest level could alleviate the problem of illiteracy. Teachers should emphasize mastery of the alphabet in class before teaching children how to read, "they should enforce the connection that children make between speaking and grammatical form, and teachers should encourage children to read out loud, according to a number of prominent educators."[xxxv]

The national assessment of educational progress has also offered its own solutions in its call for an all-out against illiteracy. The NAEP issued a report in which they said that special efforts must be made to ensure that all students learn the reasoning skills necessary for economic development and that disadvantaged students learn to read and write. "It urged in its report that school administrators and teachers need to explore new methods of instruction that foster high-order thinking and reasoning skills."[xxxvi]

Some experts believe that the high rate of illiteracy in the United States reflects the values that our culture now embodies. A professor of scientific communication at Baylor College, Dr. DeBakey, argues that illiteracy in the America reflects the values of the culture of this country. "This culture according to DeBakey, is one which holds entertainers of questionable talent and under-exercised intellect in higher esteem than people who exemplify literary, intelligence, and humanness."[xxxvii]

These varied opinions of the cause of literacy give pause for thought. However, no matter what the causes, whether they be socio-economic, cultural, or a breakdown of the educational system, the issue to be addressed is how we as educators and society as a whole can tackle the problem. The fact is, there have been a number of new and innovative programs developed to fight illiteracy.

The sing, spell, read, and write curriculum for teaching language skills has been getting enthusiastic reviews in pilot studies throughout the country. Part of the Christian Broadcasting Network heads up literacy project; the new program combines games, progress charts, and catchy songs to teach children and adults how to read. The program represents a return to the long outmoded phonics, or sounding out, method of teaching reading skills. Leaders work through churches, usually in the inner city, to train local teachers and supplement the curriculum already in use at the targeted schools. "With 27 million, or three-fourths of the country's unemployed, unable to read a newspaper or write a check, the C.B.N. believes that the time has come to reevaluate teaching methods, and this is a prime example."[xxxviii]

The public and religious sectors are not the only ones fighting the war against illiteracy, though. The fight has become one in which broad segments of society have become involved with, particularly the private sector. The president of Encyclopedia Britannica, in an address before the IBM media industry executive conference, pointed out that remedial programs that exist reach only 10 percent of the 27 million needing help. According to Mr. Wier, computer technology can come to the aid of America's faltering education system.

Software that teaches problem solving and enhances analytical thinking provides valuable job skills. Although computer-based learning may have some shortcomings, research shows that computer instruction can boost learning 10 to 40 percent and can improve long-term retention when combined with teacher assistance. "As a curriculum supplement, computers also improve student's attitudes."[xxxix]

There are obviously a number of methods that can be employed to fight illiteracy. Whether it is to go back to old-fashioned educational values, as Hirsch would subscribe to, or using innovative programs such as the heads-up program that C.B.N., has implemented, or through the use of computer technology, as Wier advocates, the point is that the modern educator must adapt whatever methods work for them in fighting the battle against illiteracy.

Not only must the government come up with more funds to enhance the literacy level in this country, but local communities, parents groups, retired educators, and clergy all must work together to develop programs that will reach as many of the 27 million functional illiterates that reside in the United States. The future of this country is at stake. The more illiterates there are in this country, the more the inability for the U.S. to progress as an advanced technological society. This will create a society composed not only of illiterates, but a larger problem as well. It must be noted that illiteracy is not a problem of the U.S. alone; more than 800 million illiterates live in developing countries throughout the world. These figures are representative of the social conditions that go hand-in-hand with illiteracy, poverty, malnutrition, illness, and infant mortality. "Educational improvement is essential to achieving world health."[xl]

CHAPTER 3
EDUCATION AND MINORITIES

Over the past hundred years, the United States has developed an educational system that is supposed to provide all people with an education, and in turn, obtain an education that will allow them to advance within society. The educational system in this country has evolved over the centuries from one that provided education to only the wealthy to the establishment of a public school system that would allow for all people, entitling them to free and quality education.

In order to advance in society economically, as well as socially, it has been traditionally viewed that obtaining an education was fundamental for advancement. This is seen through the experience of immigrants who landed on the shores of the United States at the end of the last century and the early part of this century.

The immigrants, largely from Eastern Europe, knew that in order to make it in this land of golden opportunity, they would have to learn the language, customs, and culture of this country. In order to be accepted into society, these immigrant groups, including Jews, Italians, and Irish, knew they would have to obtain an education, which would result in better jobs, more money, and eventually, hopeful acceptance.

This view was successful, by and large, as there have been thousands of success stories of immigrants who have risen to the top because they obtained an education. However, the educational system is presently undergoing many changes, and in many opinions, is undergoing a crisis. The student population in urban areas is changing and is now largely comprised of minority students, Blacks and Hispanics. As the demographics of the student population changes, educational priorities and methods should change as well.

The promise of upward social mobility and a good education is no longer present for the children of minorities. Educators must find a way to better educate poor Black and Hispanic children or risk condemning them to lives of chronic unemployment and alienation from society. Current educational reforms concentrate on instruction and curriculum, but these strategies assume that all children are equally prepared to perform in an academic environment. In reality, many poor minority children enter the school without adequate preparation because they are raised in an atmosphere that is at odds with mainstream expectation. Schools must therefore make an effort to address the special needs of developing children, especially those from marginal homes, while at the same time improving relations with parents.

Unlike the early immigrant groups who had the opportunities to move upwards, today's immigrants from Latin countries, along with Black Americans, are being stifled and frustrated. The schools are degenerating, and there are no apparent incentives for these children to succeed in school.

In his report on school segregation, James Coleman stated that minority schools have been demonstrated repeatedly to lag considerably behind schools serving a predominately white student body. As a result, by the time a student graduates from a minority high school, he/she may, according to the so-called Coleman Report, be educated only to the degree that a ninth-grade student in a white school has reached. Again, the Coleman Report stated that in the metropolitan northeast, high school students in grade twelve were shown to lag an average of 3.3 years behind the average white student, and this figure takes into account the many Black students who are known to have left school.

In another study on school desegregation, John Stanfield points out that while there are many Black students who manage to study diligently and score considerably higher than the average student on standardized tests, it must be conceded that the average Black high school graduate has received an education that is woefully deficient, even in the northeast.

In fact, there are numerous controversies concerning standardized tests. Some educators believe that the Scholastic Aptitude Test and the American College Testing are sexually and racially biased, because girls score lower than boys, and Blacks and Hispanics score lower than whites. However, there are other experts who believe there is little evidence of bias. The tests, according to some experts, are carefully examined for signs of prejudice, and questions that can be singled out as examples of inherent prejudice are rare. These experts believe that variation in test scores along racial lines are a symptom of the larger problem in society, and that the effort being applied to correcting those tests would be better applied to correcting unequal educational opportunity.

The problem of children of minority background is compounded by the fact that, in many school systems, subjects taught are not necessarily these which prove helpful to the individual. This of course is a problem that affects both Black and Hispanic students. The problem is further compounded by the fact that these students are more likely than white middle-class students to hail from culturally deprived homes.

Since these inequalities in education and other aspects of daily life are, in fact, so persuasive, it can be seen that Blacks and Hispanics do not partake of the so-called "American Dream" as members of the white majority. The dilemma that Hispanics face in this country is discussed in an article by R. Rodriguez. As the author points out, Hispanics want to be part of America, and the American Dream, but they don't want to give up their past. The Latin American culture looks to the past, while the United States stands as the opposing New World experiment, offering the promise of rebirth and separation from the past. Latin America, meanwhile, offers a fullness of life and a passion that America yearns for. This dilemma is further illustrated by a dream recounted by a ten–year-old Hispanic boy in Albuquerque, New Mexico. The dream concerned the boy's anxiety about his teacher, who had a low opinion of his academic ability. The boy faced the problem common among Spanish-speaking Americans who want to be part of the United States but want to retain their native value, customs, and language.

Cultural differences affect the education of Black Americans, as well. One particular response to the problem of educating Black students, which was more prevalent some five to ten years ago, is that of Black English. Since Black Americans are unique in that they arrived on these shores in slavery and experienced centuries of pervasive racism, it is argued that their attitudes towards education and towards the use of the language itself differs from that of the majority culture. The effect of this reasoning is to the onus for failing to absorb the curriculum upon Black themselves, leading to its being criticized by those who see it as another instance of blaming the victim. John Chambers argues in his article, "Black English," is it Black Children who have special problems, or is it American educational institutions that have special problems because of their refusal to adequately educate Black Children?

The minority child does have special needs that the educational system in the United States must address. These special needs include remedial coursework, tutoring, special counseling, etc. All these programs will affect the child's progress in the educational system. As the educational programs in this country have been slow, in many cases, to respond to these needs, the Black and Hispanic child is definitely affected in that his/her future choices will be limited.

Due to the various cultural differences that minority children face, and the lack of proper responses on the part of the educational system in the United States, it is imperative for minority groups, Blacks and Hispanics, to adjust their attitudes towards education. Adults must show young people the importance of fighting for a good education. Adults must become much more active in their child's education.

For example, parents must know their child's teacher, they should be able to identify every local education official involved with shaping the goals and values of the children in the community, and they must make themselves visible through such institutions as the local P.T.A.

At the same time, public education officials must also rise to the challenge of preparing children for the future. They can do this by insuring that there are effective principals, good teacher-principal relationships, formal parental involvement, and flexible funding that can be used in developing enrichment programs where needed. Additionally, whenever youngsters express doubt about the value of education, adults should be prepared to counter those doubts.

Amid the problems that face the minority community, in regards to education, there is progress being made. Throughout the United States, model programs have been developed, studies have been conducted, all to redirect the goals of educators to address the very problem so far discussed in this paper.

For example, amid the crack houses and gang violence of Seattle's Central Area, the Zion Christian School does provide a food education while providing a warm Christian atmosphere for 420 Black students from pre-school through eighth grade.

Principal Doug Wheeler and his teaching staff, most of whom are members of the Zion United House of Prayer, stress discipline, community, and the importance of spotlighting each child's skills. These teachers must contend with low pay, a decrepit building, and the turbulence of the inner city. However, they are committed teachers and are dedicated to the city's children, ensuring that they receive an education that will help them succeed.

This type of effort is being seen throughout the country in the public as well as private school systems. Over the past few years, educators have been making an assertive effort to reach the children and impress upon them the importance of a quality education. For example, the principle of George Washington Preparatory High School in Los Angeles has been urging Black people to believe that education is their salvation and to identify behaviors that must be adopted by public schools. He has been also urging civic leaders to create a better system for monitoring schools. His recommendations include that all schools should have teachers teach certain skills regardless of their subject area. He also suggests that a non-violent curriculum be developed that would teach pacifism at all grade levels; provide a parent-community support system; offer parent education workshops; develop peer counseling programs; operate Saturday tutorial programs; establish certain mandatory rules; offer a nurturing atmosphere; and make an effort to rescue male Black students. In essence, the above is his prescription for saving the minority child from a life of poverty and helplessness.

A common theme that is being enacted throughout the country is the necessity to involve the parents, children, and entire community in the educational process. James P. Comer, Associate Dean of the medical school at Yale University in New Haven, Connecticut, has been involved in efforts to boost the educational performance of Blacks and other minority students in impoverished inner-city areas. He has participated in a study of two elementary schools in New Haven that rose from being ranked thirty-second and thirty-third to third and fourth. Comer believes that the key to academic improvement is cooperation among parents, teachers, and school administrators.

As stated before, the problems that face Blacks in the educational system face Hispanics as well. Some Hispanics who are working toward increasing the presence of Hispanics in higher education are urging educators to eliminate marginalization, exclusion, and alienation, and to ensure that all U.S. institutions reflect the diversity of U.S. society.

Overall, there must be a concerted effort to refocus the American educational system. Urban areas are suffering tremendously in regards to proper schools, qualified teachers, decent school buildings, enough school supplies, etc. The curriculum within the inner city schools must reflect the needs of the community that it serves. A community outreach program must be developed in all areas to involve parents, encourage participation in their child's activities, and ensure that their children are attending schools. Black and Hispanic children must be exposed to the success that is available to them if they receive an education. Bringing in successful minority individuals, who have attained the American Dream, to talk to children, is just one way in which to impress upon the children the value of an education. At the same time, the quality of education in these areas must improve.

One final word involving temperament and teaching. Teachers should be alerted to the uniformities as well as to the differences in every class. This may not prove to be as simple as it sounds; simply, every teacher is not psychologically equipped to be that aware. Any group that is taught is bound to be composed of phlegmatic as well as explosive personalities. "Teaching will not only gain from the recognition of these types; it may succeed or fail because of a teacher's sensitive or dull reaction to these characteristics."[xli] If there exists one key to teaching, it is understanding the role of temperament. If an atmosphere of psychological security is to be had, the teacher must be able to cope with his own temperament as well as with the temperament of the student.

We now come to the issue of overall teacher responsibilities. It seems reasonable to believe that the "healthy teacher personality will have to become less threatened by the idea of change."[xlii] This will have to be accomplished to such an extent that change becomes second nature. Change will have to be accepted or rejected not on any "emotional basis, but rather on the basis of rational behavior."[xliii] If this is worked out effectively, change will become something to work with creatively rather than a harsh, external force. In essence, the teacher should control the course of change so that there results a development of abilities.

However, the fact remains that a teacher can not be expected to shape the minds of the young if he does not see his own relationship to the forces of change. A teacher can not be responsible unless he accepts the observation that all things are in a state of change and renewal. The mature personality is able to put all of this in perspective.

Up until this point we have covered the wider angles of personality development with references to the teacher personality. Such ideas have been rather abstract, but nevertheless, they contain a somewhat universal characteristic lending toward the development of a sound educational system. Now I will mention those references that deal specifically with teacher characteristics.

In an article by R.L. Turner, he states that teachers who appeared to have warm personalities were capable of obtaining positive changes in their students. Also, these teachers were noticed as being primarily child centered. On the other hand, "those teachers who took over the classroom in a business-like manner and who showed a high degree of organization tended to depress any changes in the creativity content of the child."[xliv]

"Another study done by Wozencraft reveals that the concept of personality is important to successful teaching, but he is unable to make clear its exact function."[xlv] Wozencraft feels that those within the educational system should hire those teachers with pleasant personalities. He states that it is difficult to attempt change in those personalities already hired.

The final study was done by J.A. Del Popolo. His study takes on a psychological point of view in that he makes reference to basic psychological needs. Del Popolo feels that the certain psychological needs are translated into behavior patterns. These patterns become potent influences on the student's social growth. This idea fits in with the self concept principle that was mentioned earlier. Once the teacher become comfortable with his own identity, the student should encounter little difficulty with his own social patterns. As with Wozencraft, the exact relationship was not made clear. However, Del Popolo did make a point to emphasize the development of personality traits in teaching.

CHAPTER 4
PROBLEMS IN EDUCATING MINORITY STUDENTS

Over twenty years ago, a citywide teachers strike in New York brought forth the issue of whether or not to decentralize the public school system. At the time, a pilot project sponsored by the Ford Foundation, a local board, was up in the Ocean Hill-Brownsville section of Brooklyn. The school board soon clashed with the United Federation of Teachers when the board tried to dismiss several teachers. The situation deteriorated into a nasty dispute that pitted many blacks against the union, whose leadership was predominantly Jewish.

The aftermath of this racially tense teachers strike was the eventual decentralization of the school system. The main reasons for decentralizing the school system was the belief that more attention would be made towards minority educational needs, along with what many believed would be a more manageable, less bureaucratic school system.

In recent months, the issue of decentralization has been raised once more. What has brought the issue to the forefront are various scandals that have emerged around New York. Charges of drug abuse, nepotism, embezzlement, and fraud in the various school districts.

The public, who may have been totally unaware of how the New York school system is run, is now aware that there is a decentralized school system, one which relegated control to local community boards. It is the power of these boards to run the schools, and allocate funds as they see fit, according to the needs of their community. The question that arises is whether or not the children of New York city are being served properly, as more and more allegations arise concerning financial abuse.

There are thirty-two school districts in New York, with each community board having a certain amount of autonomy over their districts. The Board of Education headquarters, on Livingston Street, is responsible for overseeing and monitoring the job of the local boards. However, as more and more scandals are disclosed, it is clear that there is no monitoring occurring, and that essentially each school board lives by its own code and rules. In evaluating the decentralization issue, it must be determined whether the minority population of the city of New York is being deprived a proper education because of a system that appears to be running unchecked.

To understand the decentralization issue and how it impacts upon the minority population of New York City, a historical perspective must be provided concerning the implementation of such a school system. In the late 1960s, community control advocate groups increasingly saw the professional power of the educators, exercised through their strong teachers' union and supervisory associations, as working against the public interest. "A prevailing point of view among these advocates was that educators had a monopoly over definitions of professionalism (what should be taught, how, who should evaluate the schools, and by what means) and had consolidated their power over the running of the New York City schools to such a point that they seemed increasingly unresponsive to legitimate demands of citizen groups for improved education. This view was particularly prevalent in poor black areas of the city."

These advocate groups saw the central bureaucracy as the enemy and made their main goal the decentralization of the New York City school system into a series of small community school districts. The plan was that each district would be governed by an elected community school board that would hold the educators of their district accountable for the quality of education there and would have significant power over budget, staffing, and program decisions. The benefits of decentralization, according to the advocates, would be: accountability of the educators to their constituencies; more parent and community participation in educational decision making; increasing educational innovation; a better relation of schools to communities in curriculum and staffing and in program linkages to outside agencies; more jobs within the school system for district residents; the development of more local-level leadership; improved legitimacy of the schools; and ultimately improved student performance.

Essentially the goal of the advocated was what they termed "ethnic succession." Historically, the New York City schools, like many other big city schools cities, experiences waves of ethnic migrations. In the 1950s, the education system was dominated by the Irish, followed by increasing numbers of Jewish educators. As more and more Blacks and Hispanics entered the school system in the 1960s, they demanded more entry into system. The minority population was demanding more participation and control over the education of their children, and according to them, this was not happening, as there was a closed elite of educators controlling the Board of Education.

Eventually, with the help of the Civil Rights Commission and the growing number of community advocates, the City of New York realized that maybe the centralized school system was no longer effective. The arguments that the advocates hurled concerning the ills of a centralized bureaucracy were finally heeded, and the school system was redesigned to meet the advocated demands. The advocates truly believed that the minority population would receive a better education in a decentralized system, that less corruption could occur in such a system, and that educators would be less politicized in a decentralized system, therefore not allowing for nonprofessional practices, which in turn were blamed for poor student performance.

Basically, the community advocates truly believed that decentralization of the school system would cure all the ills and provide once and for all quality education to all students in New York City, not just the middle class and upper middle class population.

As one looks back at twenty-plus years of decentralization, one sees that the dreams did not become reality. In hindsight, of course, it is easier to say that these advocates were quite naive in their assumptions; however, one can only learn from experience, as we have in the city of New York.

What has happened in New York, as stated earlier, is a series of scandals that highlight the ineffectiveness of decentralization. One example is School Board 9, which covers part of the Bronx, a poor district along the southwestern edge. Interestingly, according to officials, there have been allegations in this district of mismanagement since 1974, yet nothing has been done. In 1988, the entire board of District 9 was suspended after a grand jury began investigating charges that some board members had used and sold drugs, stolen school equipment, extorted money from principals and teachers, and used school employees to do outside political work. Except for the drug charges, the allegations in 1974 were exactly the same.

School District 9 is a prime example of what many say has gone wrong with decentralization. It is a district whose population is 95 percent Black and Hispanic, and controls 33 elementary and junior high schools. This district has a budget of over 100 million which falls under the control of the local board members.

Over the years, a state audit has found that District 9 was involved in improper hiring, widespread misspending, and millions of dollars in expenditures that could not be accounted for. There was a 3.5 million school lunch program mismanaged, a principal was caught smoking crack, cronyism and patronage was widespread. According to Fernando Ferrer, Bronx Borough President, "one of the great flaws of decentralization is that community control is not what it was supposed to be. The elections are only understood by technicians who reach out and produce the number of requisite votes to get elected. There's no scrutiny and no accountability; their behavior has gotten outrageous over the years."

The School Board of District 9 is no way an exception in the decentralized school system. District 21, in Southern Brooklyn, has often subordinated the educational interests of school children, particularly minority group pupils, to a broad political agenda that included the coercion of teachers for political chores, in addition to cronyism, patronage, and nepotism. In addition, the entire school board in that district is white. Other allegations have shown that under the all-white board, schools that serve heavily Black and Hispanic areas receive far fewer resources, "as desperate as toilet paper and computers, than other schools, and those schools regularly score lower on citywide mathematics and reading tests."

The example of these two districts, each which are predominantly composed of minority students, illustrate that the wishes of the earlier community advocates, these who believed decentralization would benefit minorities, were naive. There dreams have not come to fruition.

In response to the scandals that have emerged in recent years concerning the local school boards, there has been a very large response from citizens, educators, and politicians throughout the city. Amid accusations of misdeeds and mismanagement, a total of 703 candidates filed nominating petitions for 288 seats in 32 school board races in the last election, which occurred in May of 1989.

Amidst the scandal, education officials and community leaders have pushed for more community involvement in the elections in hopes of insuring that people concerned with education, not political or personal gain, would be elected. Interestingly, in the election of 1989, only 160 candidates were current members. The reason for this was that a special effort was made to encourage parents of pupils to become candidates. Community leaders wanted to avoid a repetition of the 1986 elections, in which about 70 board members elected were employees of the central Board of Education–principals, supervisors, teachers, and others. An employee could not serve on the school board in the district in which he or she worked but could serve in another district. An additional 15 or 20 board members held elected offices or elected political party positions.

As a result of such representation, and lack of community representation, the state passed, in December of 1988, a law called the Serrano Law, named after its sponsor, a Bronx state assemblyman, Jose Serrano. It prohibited school employees and elected political and party office holders from serving on school boards. The measure was intended to reduce potential conflicts of interest and end the exchange of favors, involving appointments and promotions, that was said to be going on among school employees serving on different school boards. The Serrano Law was one way that society responded to the problems that have arisen under decentralization. It is apparent that society has become concerned about the education that the students, particularly minority students, were or were not receiving under the decentralization system.

The societal response was also indicated in the results of the school board elections held in 1989. First of all, results showed that about 39,500 more people voted than in the previous election. The results show that 138, or 47.6 percent, of the 288 new board members were minority members, compared with 126, or 43.8 percent, in 1986, when the last election was held. Of the minority members, 88 are Black, 46 are Hispanic, and 4 are Asian.

These results, compared to those held in 1970, the first election under centralization, show that only 77 minority members were elected, about one fourth the total. In addition, for the first time since the implementation of decentralization, the boards would have more women than men. Of the 288 members, 156, or 54.2 percent were women, compared with 140 or 48.6 percent in 1986, and 97 women, or approximately one-third, in 1970.

A little less than half the board members, or 140, are incumbents, compared with 197 incumbents elected in 1986. Thirty-one fewer incumbents sought reelection in the 1989 election than in the 1986 election. Other notable results of the election, which show societal response, are that thirty percent of the candidates identified themselves as parents of public school children, and 40 percent of those won.

Though the minority representation on the school boards is not equal to the percentage or minority students in the school system, 34 percent Black and 33 percent Hispanic, the results of the election indicate a rising percentage of all minorities. This is important to note, for hopefully a broader minority representation of Blacks, Hispanics, and Asians will aid in healing the ills of the school system and ensure that minority education will improve rather than continue to deteriorate.

Other societal responses to the crisis within the decentralized school system is the growing support for drug tests for suspect school employees. As a result of Principal Matthew Barnwell's arrest for crack, the Central School Board has moved swiftly to implement some form of drug testing. Granted, there is opposition by union and civil libertarians; nonetheless, the late commissioner Green, along with past Board of Education President Wagner, have realized the necessity of drug testing. What arose out of the Barnwell arrest was the disclosure that Mr. Barnwell had been suspended three times by the local school board since 1975 for chronic lateness and absenteeism without explanation. Yet he was consistently reinstated, with the final consequences being his arrest for crack. Wagner and Green again feel that more action must be taken by the Central Board to prevent such incidents and to supervise errant local boards. The Barnwell incident was just one of many that illustrated how local boards were running without any supervision. A principal, particularly a minority principal, should serve as a role model for minority students. Unfortunately, a corrupt and inept school board refused to intervene, recognize that Mr. Barnwell had a problem, never recommended drug treatment for him, and created a devastating situation for students.

Presently, there are moves under way to study possible changes in the school system. There are very few individuals who deny that decentralization has failed in its expectations and that a restructuring is needed. Lawmakers and educators are watching closely how school administrations in places such as Chicago and Dade County, areas with high minority populations, are revamping their systems. They are decentralizing their systems; however, they are doing it down to the smallest possible unit, the school. "It's something we should consider," says Joseph Shenker, president of the Bank Street College of Education. We all think the parochial and private schools are successful, and one of there reasons is that all decisions are made at the school level. This is what is commonly referred to as a base management form of education. This form of decentralization, to the smallest possible size as feasible, seems to be the most advantageous type of system, according to many educators. If the concern is the proper education of minorities, the more input from minorities, the better the education, is the prevailing line of thought.

What has been discovered in this examination of a decentralized school system is that no system is exempt from corruption, nepotism, fraud, cronyism, patronage, and drug abuse. If there are people who are able to steal and mismanage millions of dollars of funds that are meant for the students, these people will always find a way to accomplish their goals, if we let them.

It does not appear that decentralization in and of itself is at fault for the poor education that minority students are receiving. It is the control, or lack of control, that these local boards are subject to. There is no accountability, no monitoring, and no effective devices put into place to prevent these scandalous occurrences.

First of all, school boards should be so structured that a fair representation of the population will be on the board. The school boards can be made smaller, though I am not sure, or a school by school basis. The boards, though, must have a checks and balances system, in which independent auditors monitor the activities of the board.

Secondly, social services should be provided to educators, students, parents, and board members alike. If there is reason to believe that there is a substance abuse problem, then the individual should be counseled, rather than ignored, for more harm will be done to the individual and the student if this occurs.

The community must become more involved in the educational process. It is very important that the P.T.A. or some like group is an active one. It is important that school board members, along with educators, seek out parental involvement. Regular meetings at individual schools must be held to let parents hear what is going on, to let them express their ideas, and to provide some interaction between teacher and parent.

If students see that their parents care about their education, they will respond in a positive way. This parental involvement should be carried over in the homes, as well. Parents must insure that their children do their homework. Setting aside study periods at home is a good idea. Parents should also listen to their children read out loud, to help them improve their reading skills. Parents must always be aware of what their children are studying and show an active interest.

In addition, local school boards should develop literacy programs, particularly in minority areas. Many parents do not speak English or have had a poor educational history. If students are to succeed, then it should be a community effort. Make education fun, while encouraging the entire community, parents, aunts, uncles, grandparents, to participate in the school system. Go to meetings, participate in classes, make education a family affair. In this way, regardless of the system in place, minority students will receive a proper education.

A review of this literature suggests the desirability of conducting further studies in the same direction with a view toward developing a more explicit hypothesis.

HYPOTHESIS

I am trying to determine which behavior patterns of the teacher most influence the pupils' social growth. It is my belief that schools would have taken a giant step toward improvement if they had been able to detect and identify which personality traits characterize effective teachers. Also, if they had been able to predict which individuals would exhibit these traits before they were to go on the job.

I think that a study such as this would add to an understanding of which type of people would be successful in teaching. If this is determined, then the development of working with material exactly the same; though they might appear to have basically the same objectives, they will both present two very different pictures to any classroom observer. As a result, different teachers will appeal to different children.

There seems to be a considerable amount of information which suggests that particular personality characteristics have a somewhat discernible influence on learning, behavior, and the overall adjustment of students. However, it seems that the premise of a well-adjusted person making a better teacher has not been demonstrated consistently. The accepted fact seems to be that an effective teacher should be paired with a particular teaching situation. The so-called "non-effective" teacher also has a particular situation with which to be matched. "It is quite possible that a teacher who does a remarkable job in one area will do a poor job in another."[44]

Teachers are individuals having their own particular needs just as the student. It is fortunate when a type of interaction occurs. Here both personalities come together, resulting in the enhancement of the two. However, this is a seldom occurrence.

To illustrate the type of thinking that is done in connection with the personality idea, let us look at one dimension and follow its implications. Several studies have tried to isolate a personality variable that is known as the as the "tolerance of ambiguity." People who have a high tolerance level tend to be comfortable in unstructured situations. They also seem to be willing to let things develop and to have little need to exert close control over situations or other people. They appear to be rather flexible and permissive when dealing with others. At the opposite end, we have those with a low tolerance level. These people seem to be more comfortable when situations are clear cut and are organized and planned in a careful manner. In summary, "they are more rigid personalities, most often looking for clear-cut answers."[45]

The teacher fitting into the first type will most likely be the one to encourage such things as creativity, critical thinking, and various other activities. This teacher sets high standards and goals for the students; therefore, the children feel a sense of creativity and responsibility. Thus, there is a wider range for self-actualization and the development of a more positive concept. In one study done by Robert Rosenthal and L. Jacobson, it was indicated that whatever a teacher expects from a student, he will probably get. The need for the teacher to "believe in the children's ability to succeed as certainly supported by their work."[46] In the book entitled *Teacher and Child*, by Haim G. Ginott, he goes beyond the theoretical approach and offers a model for a language of acceptance and compassion, words that convey feelings, responses that change moods, statements that invite good will, answers that bring insight, replies that radiate respect, and in general, a language that lingers lovingly. Ginott's suggestions are designed to increase a students' sense of self pride and to enhance the quality of life in the classroom.

The teacher in the second category is most likely to emphasize responses, routine situations, and controlled teaching. As expected, some children will do well under one approach; some will do just as well under the second approach. It should be kept in mind the fact that most students lie somewhere in between the two methods. But, obviously, most children will come into contact with an assortment of teachers as perceived along this dimension.

In one study done by I.G. Ryans, the Minnesota Teacher Attitude Inventory (MTAI) was used to measure the attributes of teachers. It is more representative of the views of elementary teachers than of secondary school teachers. In this test it is possible to identify those teachers who seem to be stimulating and businesslike in the classroom but whose relationships with their students show little warmth.

Several ideas were introduced because of this particular study. These were the following hypotheses:

1. The attributes, abilities, and values of a teacher determine the method and style of teaching.

2. The style of a teacher is one factor that is perceived by the student. This perception is decreased beyond the elementary school level.

3. Common elements of the faculty as a group have a stronger effect on the school environment. Teachers are hired to reinforce the existing pattern.

4. A teacher will change a student's personality development only if his teaching style influences the press felt by the student. "The personality of the student will be the determining factor as far as what type of change will occur."[47]

Patterns of Observed Behavior (Teacher)	Teacher Response Measures Related to Observed Patterns
Pattern X	Measures Related to Pattern X
warm, understanding,	1. Tendency to choose the

friendly versus	more friendly activities
aloof, egocentric,	
restricted	2. Amount of permissivenes favored
	3. Tendency to choose the stimulating activities
	4. Verbal understanding
	5. Emotional stability
	6. Tendency to have favorable opinions of students
Pattern Y	Measures Related to Pattern Y
Responsible, businesslike,	1. Tendency to choose the
systematic versus	more
evading, unplanned, slipshod	businesslike, systematic activi ties
Pattern Z	Measures Related to Pattern Z
Stimulating, surgence more imaginative	1. Tendency to choose the
versus dull, routine	stimulating
	activities

Adapted from D.G. Ryans. <u>Characteristics of Teachers</u>. Washington, D.C.: American Council on Education, 1960.

Teachers are most interested in knowing what attitudes and what types of behaviors are likely to produce the best results in the classroom. The issue concerning an analysis of the effective teacher has proceeded in several directions. Many theorists have discussed the consequences of learning emerging from various teacher personality characteristics, attitudes, and values as they interact with students. Several of these theorists have reported their findings as classical studies. These include Amidon and Flanders (1963); Anderson (1937, 1946); Barr (1961); Beilin (1959); Jersild (1940); Lewin, Lippitt, and White (1939); Lippitt and White (1958); Ryans (1959, 1960); and Wickman (1928).

Jersild was interested in those characteristic of teachers who were liked best as compared with those teachers who were most disliked by their students. Children were found to prefer teachers who were kind, cheerful, natural, and warm. Second, fair, consistent, and respected. Third, those teachers who were well groomed and generally attractive. And, fourth, "those who were helpful, democratic, and enthusiastic."

Two other studies, done by Anderson (1937), and Lewin, Lippitt, and White (1939), are prime examples of teachers displaying attitudinal characteristics in creating an atmosphere in which the group functions. Anderson stated that hostile teachers would affect the student adversely, while the opposite type would facilitate the personal and social adjustment of their students. In his observation of teacher-pupil behavior, Anderson defines "dominating" behavior as using force, threats, and rigid insistence on conformity. "Integrative" behavior was defined by several supporting and positive descriptions such as teacher approval, interest in pupil activity, and understanding. As a rule, it was found that the integrative teacher produced children with integrative behavior. Also, there were more indications of spontaneity and initiative in these students. The children in the dominative class were more resistant, paid less attention in the classroom, and engaged in such activity as whispering, talking in class, and becoming easily distracted.

As a result of this study, Anderson came upon two important conclusions. First, that "integrative behavior in the teacher produces integrative behavior in the child." And, secondly, teachers do not seem to change their teaching behavior from year to year.

When teacher and pupil personalities interact, the pupil's achievement is determined. In the Powell and Feifer study (1960), this question was taken up. Three teacher personality traits were taken up long with four pupil personalities. These were compared with measures of student achievement, teacher knowledge, and classroom ratings. With results that were similar to the Anderson study, it was found that teachers with integrative behavior were the most effective with every type of student. On the other hand, those with low integrative behavior were the least effective. Teachers who were intellectuals but who made use of defense mechanisms in the classroom were found to be nonstimulating with students who were non-conformers, but brought about higher achievement scores in students who were the supposed conformers. We can assume that the personality of the teacher is strongly connected to the achievement of students.

The second study done by Lewin, Lippitt, and White (1939) did not produce a shocking conclusion but, nevertheless, is regarded as a classic experiment because of its similarity to the school situation. The experiment consisted of several groups of five-member classes in which ten-year-old boys were instructed to make such objects as paper masks, airplanes, and carved objects.

The groups were then separated into three distinct leadership styles; the first, autocratic, the second, democratic, and the third, laissez faire. The leader of the autocratic group stated the objectives of his program and directed all the activities. The leader of the democratic group attempted to be non-dominating in his decision making. Under the laissez faire system, no directions were given and the leader did not work with the other boys in trying to determine a goal.

After the data was interpreted, it was found that in the authoritarian group the boys became extremely dependent upon the leader. They also failed in an effort to initiate group activity. They also seemed to show an attitude of aggressiveness and rebellion toward the leaders. The laissez faire group exhibit complete confusion. Discontent seemed to be the prevalent attitude. Finally, the democratic group showed qualities of friendliness, sociability, and cooperation. The quality and quantity of the boys' work was then looked over. It was found that the work done by the democratic group appeared to be superior to the others. Also, when the leaders no longer attended the meetings, the level of work dropped, but the level in the democratic group learned to work in a cooperative way.

It can be inferred that the perception of a situation by a student and his personality behavior determine what kind of behavior will follow. The effectiveness of this lies in the student's acceptance of a particular mode of instruction.

Situation	Authoritarian	Democratic	Laissez Faire
Teacher Present	50%	50%	30%
Teacher Absent	15%	50%	50%
Teacher Returns	60%	40%	20%

Adapted from Lewin, Lippitt, and White (1939).

A final word should be said about male and female teachers in relation to their view of criteria. This criteria involved student adjustment. The teachers selected in this particular study were to choose three of their best students and three of their least-adjusted students. This was to be done without considering sex differences. Female attitudes were brought to the surface when they assessed a well-adjusted student by character traits such as humility. They also stated that a negative adjustment was made by those students who did not get along with the teacher, as well as those who were discipline problems. The male teachers seemed to display somewhat different attitudes as to what a well or badly adjusted pupil was like. They termed the adjusted student as those who were trustworthy and dependable, also, those students who were able to solve problems with good judgment. The better students were expected to have a much greater degree of self confidence as more successful students should follow. I expect to find that teachers who exhibit qualities of achievement, autonomy, affiliation, and endurance will most effectively foster maximum growth in the student.

Economic and social forces are increasingly diminishing the effectiveness of the family in shaping the personality. I believe that most behavior is learned. Socially acceptable behavior can be taught. Children learn by limitation because they are motivated to do so. If they experience success rather than the frustration of failure, it will result in positive motivation. A warm, friendly, and secure teacher can accomplish this.

Reversely so, I expect to find that those teachers who do not follow these characteristics will encounter failure in their teaching. The qualities of aggression and dominance will only depress the student's spontaneity and enthusiasm for learning. Therefore, I expect to find that the latter group will not be capable of making the child feel secure and confident. The children, in turn, will not be willing to put forth their best efforts.

If we return ourselves to the concept that teaching is an art, we come to the realization that teaching is a highly individualized process in which the personality of the teacher, in interaction with the students, becomes a highly personal variable. Consider the problem of two teachers well as "ego strength."[50] The male teacher also commented that those students who were the least adjusted were basically more insecure than the good students.

Through a thorough review of the literature as well as other research, I have found my hypothesis to be true. The personality of the teacher has, indeed, a great amount of influence on the shaping of the young mind.

CHAPTER 5
CREATING THE LEARNING ENVIRONMENT

The premise of any learning environment is that teachers should be perpetual students of teaching. Ideally, the teacher should encourage student independence. Learning materials should be accessible. The arrangement of the classroom should be done in a manner which strengthens the desire to learn. This chapter is an instructional strategy for the classroom planner. The teacher-arranged environment has a great influence on children's lives and will, in short, determine how much, or how delightfully, a child learns.

The foundation of any learning environment is the architectural facility. Whether a box or a room or a progressive multi-leveled habitat, it is up to the teacher to dress the environment with the props of learning. If the arrangement of materials is carefully plotted, lessons will unfold with little or no help from the teacher and in this way free their hands of many managerial tasks. Ultimately, this provides children with more quality time with their teacher as they are free to help with individual projects instead of having to speak to the whole group.

By placing certain material adjacent to others, children tend to make connections on their own. Thus, material arrangement can act in a sort of partnership with the teacher and can smooth independent transitions from one activity to another. By letting the materials themselves guide the children, they learn how to be self-reliant and how to manage themselves without authoritative directions. The four steps a teacher should embrace are: one, special organization; two, provisions for learning; three, material arrangement; and four, organization of a system that can be followed differently by each child. The teachers need to acquaint themselves with a conceptual framework of how to best use space to promote learning.

It is very important to think of space in terms of a child's eye view. The best method of seeing space as a child does is to actually crouch down and take a look. It is their world that the teacher is organizing, not that of an adult.

As an example of what might seem progressive special planning actually ruffles the philosophy of education when three teachers decide to make invisible boundaries between what should have been three separate classrooms and call it open education. Because the students are not clear where they belong exactly in this environment it becomes counter productive. Since it is impossible to know which teacher to listen to, as three are lecturing on the topic African Culture simultaneously, concentration breaks down, and children break out in conversations between themselves. In this case, what might appear progressive and innovative in terms of open space doesn't facilitate, and indeed hinders, the child's "ability to learn."

Chapter Two addresses the fact that many classrooms are a good deal larger than a teacher's initial perception. A teacher should not automatically preclude his space from that of the students' (if the classroom is particularly cramped). Even the surface of the teacher's desk can serve as a stopgap work area. Another trick is to put all the furniture on wheels so that new spaces can be created in the blink of an eye. In general, the teacher should be as flexible as possible in his thinking about space and how it can be manipulated to best suit the children. It is often observed that many children move furniture about to promote conditions they are most comfortable in. For instance, some wish to be within touching distance of others. Placing children face to face invites interaction, while private space shelters individuals from the stimulation of others. A good way to help visualize special possibilities is to draw a floor plan with cutouts representing furniture; moving the model furniture around one can observe bottlenecks and previously unnoticed free areas.

It is very important to take up as much space as possible in the classroom environment, as it has been postulated and proven that overcrowding can constrain behavior. When people get in each other's way there is undue stress created, and the process of learning is severely, if not totally, disrupted. If the special potential of a particular space is maximized, the density of the population will at least seem less, and the "business of learning will be free to carry on."[51]

Chapter Three stresses that the wrong arrangement of furniture, and therefore space, may cause undesired behavior. Environment messages may need to be altered. A unit is the term given to space where specific activities are intended to occur. A potential unit–or idle space–if rearranged and/or provisioned with learning props, may prove more constructive activity than horseplay, say, in an empty coat room.

It is absolutely crucial that the surrounding space of two different units do not overlap. When one child drifts into the surrounding space of a unit where he does not belong, an unagreeable level of friction is liable to erupt as the two conflicting activities clash.

The way to have one unit skirt another is to have well-panned paths laid out so that the children are seemingly self-directed away from units they have nothing to do with. Besides taking in the view from a child's eye level, it is instrumental to draw "sketch maps" and in this way chart the movement of the children to determine dead space (where children tend to slide and roughhouse) and other problem areas.

Joseph C. Grannis defines different schools as different sorts of society. If we focus, then, on the "factory" school, where the children are conditioned to work on exactly the same project as his neighbor, for hours and hours on end, the notion of paths drifting into opposing units is not even a consideration as each unit, by definition in a factory school is working on the identical project and therefore–even if the children were free to move about–there is no real possibility for friction. "Although some children resist the monotony, the 'factory' school conditions the individual to simply punch the clock each day and stay put through hours of tedium."[52]

Chapter Four outlines the basic framework of provision in the classroom. If the provisions are stationed well enough the children will be able to sustain productive activity independent of the teacher. There is a noticeable amount of unfocused behavior when a handful of children finish their assignment ahead of their peers. Children need, therefore, the raw materials to experiment independently. They need tools to explore ideas, information sources, adequate work space, and proper display facilities. The raw material should be changed often to impart variety. Some raw materials might be recordings, various media forms, information about living things, as well as the living things themselves. As much information as can be interestingly presented with varying sources, all with the goal of increasing knowledge, should be the ultimate driving force of provisions. Different information sources require different skills; in this way children are stimulated to use a wide range of skills.

Displays are necessary for children to facilitate sharing their work with others. There are many examples of displays; bulletin boards, racks, frames, and easels are the most common. The teacher should make a checklist of raw materials, tools, information sources, containers, work spaces, and display facilities to see which need work.

A playground designer is confronted with a similar task as the teacher in a classroom: how to entertain vastly different individuals, and how to get them to act on their own, without direction. The three major goals of the playground designer were to offer varied opportunities for active play, to promote interaction among children, and to offer places to accommodate quite play and privacy. "Tire structure provided the means for active play, he developed multiple ways for children to leave a particular activity (or arrive at it) for interaction, and he had domes and things to provide a bit of sanctuary for those kids who preferred privacy."[53]

Chapter Five begins by stating that learning is directly related to provisions. One way to increase the amount of provisions is to trade with other educators. This increases variety and therefore learning. Another good idea is to have children label all the provisions, a good activity to build vocabulary. The greater the amount of provisions, the greater the learning possibilities. For example, to really study frogs the teacher might provide books on frogs, slides on frogs, a diagram of a frog, a filmstrip, and finally a frog itself. The higher the complexity of the provisions, the longer the attention spans. The more complex, the more choices offered. Provisions should be drawn on from the community; seashells from the shore, odd-lot stores, garage sales, surplus yards, and the yellow pages are all fine places to begin.

In secondary schools it has been studied that the classroom (perhaps irregardless of provisions) is fifteen times safer than the hallways and thirty times safer than the restrooms. In short, highly supervised areas (provisions are a built-in supervision if they are well planned) are "safer than unsupervised places like halls and bathrooms where there are no provisions whatsoever."[54]

The arrangement of materials (says Chapter Six) must be made appealing before kids will use them. Inventive holders serve not only to organize materials but to entice children. Check how the displays look from a child's eye level. Make sure they are well spaced and adequately visible. Create a checklist to determine which students worked with what materials when.

John Dewey, when looking for desks, was moved by what one salesman said about his wares. He said they were not what he wanted; they were made for listening, not working. Dewey was progressive in that he knew (and articulated) the need for active education. "Active education by means of interaction with clever provisions as opposed to listening to the teacher's staid lesson is precisely what the famous educator searched for, and what the teacher who provides provisions will–if he is circumspect–attain."[55]

The distribution of materials in a decentralized pattern will promote self-direction, breadth of learning, and a longer attention span. If the provisions were always stacked the same way, unfortunate patterns would develop–crowding at certain popular provision spots, etc., and so by mixing things up one not only creates a smoother traffic flow around the room, he also stimulates children to think in new ways. For instance, soap placed beside carving tools will be thought of much differently than when placed beside a bubble pipe.

Mr. Dewey expatiates on an activity by some children whereby they made a loom and aped Navajo designs for blankets. Though the resources were limited, the children were excited by the activity because it had to do with people and was something new to them. "New provisions, in short, provide for a new kind of learning."[56]

Chapter Eight confronts the introduction of the child to literacy and declares that reflections of literacy help the child move into the world of literacy. Instead of having a table set aside for creative writing, it is more effective to have clipboards next to displays of insects, complete with labels, so that the child will decide to write on his own. Display books handsomely, covers out, or open to a nifty illustration; and supply them blank books for the kids to write in.

A study in Nashville, whereof the researcher was interested in the varying performance of students in a large classroom as opposed to a small one, determined that reading scores in the small classes were significantly higher than those in the larger ones. Whether or not the teachers in the small, experimental classes employed the creative introduction to literary described in chapter eight is not known; however, "there was certainly more chance for this sort of introduction here than in the over-populated classroom."[57]

Chapter Nine, the last, addresses the specific needs of special children and how they can benefit from environment provisions just as normal children. Generally, the same principals of promoting self-direction apply, but for the visibly impaired large signs are provided, brighter colors, and more space; spatial flow is critical for children confined to wheelchairs or encumbered by crutches. The removal, or partial alleviation, of all barriers, plus spatial organization supports, help the handicapped child negotiate his environment. Simple things, like placing provisions in the front of shelves, or providing them with handles, aid special children and grant the same sort of learning normal children enjoy.

If handicapped children can be compared to those reared in homes with parents of questionable developmental support, then by carefully adjusting the provisions and space to those of special needs, there is no reason why any child cannot develop adequately without the probability of a maladaptive developmental course "(within the reasonable limits of a child's particular handicap)."[58]

Conclusively, in spite of diverse variables and situations in school systems; Teacher characteristics and personalities are definitely associated with changes in pupil behavior. The successful teacher can take criticism and be objective in all situations, thus promoting a positive and caring atmosphere in the classroom. It was also pertinent to indicate that minority students achieved more if their teachers respected them and had faith in their ability to succeed, academically. Therefore, educational achievement among Blacks and other minorities can improve if there is cooperation between parents, teachers, and administrators. It is unequivocally clear that an understanding teacher can be an effective educator, thus providing an atmosphere which will allow the students to actualize and maximize their potential.

BIBLIOGRAPHY

Bain, Helen, Pat & Achilles, C.M., Interesting Developments on Class Size. Phi Delta Kappan May/1986.

Baun, Andrew and Koman, Stuart, Differential Response To Anticipated Crowding: Psychological Effects of Social and Spatial Density. J. Pers. Soc. Psychol. 1976, 34, 526–36.

Bowen, E., "Losing the War of Letters," Time, May 5, 1986, p. 68.

Choliar, S., "Latchkey Kids: Who are They?" Psychology Today. December, 1987, p. 12.

Coles, R., "Hispanic Dreams/American Dreams," Change. May/June, 1988, p. 12.

Comer, J. P., "Educating Poor Minority Children," Scientific American, November, 1988, p. 42.

"Community Should Provide More Support for Libraries Taking in 'Latchkey Kids," Jet, March 7, 1988, p. 42.

DeBakey, L., "Our National Priority." Vital Speeches of the Day, June 1, 1987, p. 496.

Dewey, John. The School and Society. Chicago University Press 1899.

Fields, H., "Education Department Finds Fewer Illiterates," Publishers Weekly, May 23, 1986, p. 30.

Grannis, Joseph C. The School as a Model of Society.

Harman, D., "Functional Illiteracy: Keeping Up in America," Current. September, 1986, p. 4.

"Hispanic's Higher Education's Missing People," Change May/June, 1988, p. 6.

Hylton, R.D. "Will the Class of 2000 Make the Grade?" Black Enterprise, October, 1988, p. 130.

"Improving Literacy Level is Crucial: NAEP," Phi Delta Kappan, May, 1987, P. 71.

"Judge Announces Strategy to Curb Black Illiteracy," Jet. June 30, 1986, p. 22.

Krause, K., "Gaining Ground: Poverty Programs That Work: Hammers and Nails in Mt. Winans," The Washington Monthly, April, 1986, p 21.

Laurita, H. E., "Let's Do Something About Literacy Now!" America, June 6, 1987, p. 455.
Leo, J., "Stop Blaming the Tests," U.S. News and World Report. March 20, 1989, op. 80.

Levine, K., "Children at Work," Parents, April, 1988, p. 76.

"Literacy and Well Being," World Health, March, 1986, p. 6.

Loughlin, Catherine E. and Suina, Joseph H., The Learning Environment. Teacher's College Press, New York 1982.

McCabe, S., "Problems and Solutions," The Humanist, May/June, 1986, p. 34.

McKenna, G., "Education is the Fundamental Ingredient in the Prescription for Saving Our Children," Ebony, August, 1988, p. 124.

Miller, H.G. "Heads Up for Literacy," The Saturday Evening Post, September, 1986, p. 50.

"New Efforts to Help America's Poor," Scholastic Update, (Theacher's Edition), March 23, 1987, p. 3.

Proshansky, Etta & Wolfe Maxine, The Physical Settings and Open Education. Chicago U. Press, 1975.

Ruffin, D.C., "The More to Reform Welfare," Black Enterprise, January, 1987, p. 21.
"Teachers, Parents Working Together Vital to Boosting Kid's School Achievement," Jet, December 12, 1988, p. 23.

Tuttleton, J.W., "Literacy at the Barricades," Commentary, July, 1987, p. 45.

"U.S. Hoards Food as Many Here go Hungry," Jet, September 15, 1986, p. 4.

Weinstein, Pinciotti, Changing A Schoolyard. Environment and Behavior, May 1968.

Wier, P.A., "Our Faltering Educational System." Vital Speeches of the Day, June 15, 1986, p. 523.

FOOTNOTES

[i] Donohue, G.T. and Nictern, S. Teaching the Troubled Child. New The Free Press, 1965, 87.

[ii] Telford, C.W. and Sawrey, J.M. The Exceptional Individual: Psychological and Educational Aspects. Englewood: Prentice Hall, 1967, 42.

[iii] Deese, J. and Hulse, S.H. The Psychology of Learning. New York: McGraw Hill, 1967, 5.

[iv] 4Telford, C.W. Sawrey, J.M. Educational Psychology. Boston: Allyn and Bacon, 1968, 483.

[v] A. Roe, The Psychology of Occupations. New York: John Wiley and Sons, 1959, pp 7–14.

[vi] A.T. Jersild, In Search of Self. New York: Columbia University, 1952, p. 20.

[vii] B. Massialas. Creative Encounters in the Classroom. New York: John Wiley and Sons, 1969, p7 and 263.

[viii] Op. Cit. A.T. Jersild, p.104.

[ix] Ibid., p 104.

[x] Ibid., p 107.

[xi] J. Hilderbrand, Is Intelligence Important? New York: The MacMillan Co., 1963, pp. 35–38.

[xii] Ibid., p. 43.

[xiii] J.B. Conant, The Education of American Teachers. New York: McGraw-Hill Co., 1963, p 12.

[xiv] Op. Cit. A. T. Jersild. P. 120.

[xv] Ibid., p 121.

[xvi] R. Coles. "Hispanic Dreams/American Dreams." Change. May/June, 1988, pp. 12–13.

xvii D.C. Ruffin. "The Move to Reform Welfare." <u>Black Enterprise.</u> January, 1987, p. 21.

xviii M. Kaus. "The Work Ethnic State." <u>The New Republic.</u> July 7, 1986, pp. 22-25.

xix K. Krause. "Gaining Ground: Poverty Programs that Work; Hammers and Nails in Mr. Winans." <u>The Washington Monthly</u>. April, 1986, pp. 21-23.

xx Ibid., pp. 24-26.

xxi "Community Should Provide More Support for Libraries Taking in Latchkey Kind." <u>Jet.</u> March 7, 1988, p. 37.

xxii S. Choliar. "Latchkey Kids: Who are They?" <u>Psychology Today.</u> December, 1987, p. 12.

xxiii K. Levine. "Children at Work." <u>Parents.</u> April 1988, p. 70.

xxiv R. Rodriguez. "The Fear of Losing a Culture." <u>Time.</u> July 11, 1988, p. 84.

xxv "Hispanic's Higher Education's Missing People." <u>Change.</u> May/June, 1988, p. 6.

xxvi D. Hylton. "Will the Class of 2000 Make the Grade?" <u>Black Enterprise.</u> October, 1988, pp. 122-130.

xxvii E. Bowen. "Losing the War of Letters." <u>Time</u>. May 5, 1986, p. 68.

xxviii Ibid., p. 68.

xxix Ibid., p. 68.

xxx Ibid., p. 68.

xxxi Ibid., p. 68.

xxxii S. McCabe. "Problems and Solutions." <u>The Humanist</u>. May/June, 1988, p. 34.

xxxiii J. W. Tuttleton. "Literacy at the Barricades." <u>Commentary</u>. July, 1987, p. 45.

xxxiv D. Harman. "Functional Illiteracy: Keeping up in America." <u>Current</u>. September, 1986, p. 4.

xxxv H.E. Laurita. "Let's Do Something About Literacy Now!" <u>America</u>. June 6, 1987, p. 455.

xxxvi "Improving Literacy Level is Crucial: NAEP." <u>Phi Delta Kappan</u>. May, 1987, p. 71.

xxxvii L. DeBakey. "Our National Priority." <u>Vital Speeches of the Day</u>. June 1, 1987, p. 496.

xxxviii H. G. Miller. "Heads Up for Literacy." <u>The Saturday Evening Post</u>. September, 1986, p. 50.

xxxix P.A. Weir. "Our Faltering Educational System." <u>Vital Speeches of the Day</u>. June 15, 1986, p. 523.

xl "Literacy and Well Being." <u>World Health</u>, March 1986, p. 6.
xli R.N. Snow. "Anxieties and Discontents In Teaching." <u>Phi Delta Kappa</u>, 44:23–40. 1954.

xlii Reichart. <u>Change and The Teacher New York</u>. Thomas Y. Crowell Co., 1969, p15.

xliii Ibid., p. 16.

xliv R.L. Turner. "Teacher Characteristics, Teacher Behavior, and Changes in Pupil Creativity." <u>Elementary School Journal</u>, p. 70, 1959.

xlv M. Wozencraft. "Teacher's Personality." <u>Progress Education</u>. 33:709, 1959.